SANCTUARIES OF INVENTION

ALSO BY JENNIFER RAHIM

Fiction
Songster and Other Stories
Curfew Chronicles

Poetry
Mothers Are Not the Only Linguists
Between the Fence and the Forest
Approaching Sabbaths
Redemption Rain: Poems
Ground Level

Non-Fiction
As editor (with Barbara Lalla) *Beyond Borders: Cross Culturalism and the Caribbean Canon* (2009) and *Created in the West Indies: Caribbean Perspectives on V.S. Naipaul* (2011).

JENNIFER RAHIM

SANCTUARIES OF INVENTION

PEEPAL TREE

First published in Great Britain in 2021
Peepal Tree Press Ltd
17 King's Avenue
Leeds LS6 1QS
England

© 2021 Jennifer Rahim

ISBN13: 9781845234539

All rights reserved
No part of this publication may be
reproduced or transmitted in any form
without permission

Thanks to Jeremy Poynting and the Peepal Tree team
for making this publication possible

CONTENTS

i: For the good of the change

First Crocodile's Arrival	9
Columbus's Egg, Retold	11
The Orbis Spike, 1610	12
Ibises at the Caroni Bird Sanctuary	14
Orange Turn	15
Bones	17
Gone Viral	18
Survival	19
Design	20
A Future	21
Negotiating with a Pending Earthquake	22
Haya	24

ii: mapping home (en route)

Valencia (en route)	27
Salybia	29
Balandra Poui	30
Simply, Rampanalgas	31
Cumana	33
Palm Tree Junction	34
At Toco's Depot	35
Trois Roches	36
L'Anse Noire	37
A Piece of Advice	38
Sunday Justice	39
To the Motherland	41
I Dream of Cuba	43
Homing Now to Stardust	45
On the Caroni Swamp	48
Point Cumana	51

A Movement on Time	54
A Maxi to Port of Spain	55
Wherever I Go	56

iii: saving your fire…

No / Language is a Virus	59
The Dawn-bringer's Tale, Retold	61
Soucouyant Considers Flight	62
La Diablesse Resurrect	63
Persephone to Demeter	65
Gleanings on Marianne Moore Approaching 1947	67
Releasing Judith's Lines	69
Miss Miles, Elevated	70
Remembering Anson G.	71
For Eric Roach	73
Put Away Blues	76
Legacy	78
Please Send Me Flowers	79
Loving the Daffodils	81
Returns	82

i: for the good of the change…

FIRST CROCODILE'S ARRIVAL

Everything from this day onward
will depend on this: remember –
first ancestor crocodile swam an ocean
to these Americas.
    No one forced or stole her.
No one entirely knows the why
of her leaving all behind. She swam
with the sweet ache of her mating
in her muscles
and the scent of the Nile's blue lilies
quickening with each mile.
The frangipanis were in blossom
on the other side.
    She did not know this:
multiplications surged in her blood
as she navigated mountainous waves,
and the deepest valleys, battled leviathans
that gate-keep crossings.
Conviction was the horizon's empty line –
that there will be a land to light on,
a place to make a home. Not a *paradise*
of the kind that would prefer you exiled,
would prefer that you forget your strength.
    For that arrival,
she kept afloat, treading water for rest,
    tasted salt,
relied on her tail as rudder and weapon
as she glided and paddled towards a shore
where she could ground,
and birth.
    Now, granddaughter, that you have chosen
to love, know this:
her womb was a treasury of eggs, and you
were her fought-for revelation

of the infinity we carry.
    For that possibility,
and for the worlds you, too, will deliver,
she never stopped counting on a future
long before any hatching. Hope
must always be bold
and sharpened for tomorrows.
    I pray you gain her armour:
thick skin, scaled impervious to attack,
tender underbelly that welcomes
and bleeds, a back broad enough
to carry truths
we dare not hold,
and when necessary, jaws to crack
any that conspire to beat you down.
    Remember:
dwell close to water
and love the sun. They are life.
Know when to temper your lightning moves
and stay your claws.
You are chosen – bridge
between worlds.

COLUMBUS'S EGG, RETOLD

Columbus boy, your ears must be tired ring. Tales about you run like vine through these islands. They will outlast any statue we choose to bring down – as though to blank you from sight amounts to a slate well wiped of the shadow of you. Story is another matter. No infant's game of peek-a-boo but, like salt on carili, could transform how we tell a history, when forgetting is never wholly possible, advisable or forgivable. So here's another tale about you, Mr. Christopher:

That morning, at the sight of landfall, Columbus, feeling that he deserved a treat, chanced a request for eggs and a sherry – to celebrate his luck. To his delight, one came, hard-boiled, judiciously saved from growing stale. He recalled the egg in which *he* was star. Brute genius of discovery's error, he'd smashed the base flat, so it stood on end, and won his wager. That triumph of invention was sweet vindication. Psalms rose in him; but all too soon a queen, a king and his *converso* mother, intruded. Cristóbal saw the royal supper table: fresh fruit, red wine, roasted quail *and* the vital cuts of pork – fried in prime lard. Italia and Iberia flashed before him, the thirst for a home, and the hope of no more split-living. Loyalties sparked to flame, then sputtered before the prize. *Discovery* – it could all be his!

Colombo downed his drink, peeled the shattered shell and paused to notice the dark spot like an eclipsed sun in a feathered sky. He blinked. Sliced the oval down the middle, the script unreadable. He said grace, ate uneasily, sword in scabbard. Yellow on his plate burned a fever. He chewed over his next letter home. The egg did its work. Pressure. Surf exploded meteoroids.

From the river's mouth, crocodile saw all, swished her tail and covered her stash. Colón landed and took charge. Night came. Hatchlings armoured. Sea hissed, sizzled, coiled, and swallowed itself ouroboros – again and again, a renewed arrival. Cristoforo, though, returned to Spain in chains; but they never put up any statue to mark that part (footnote, Hispaniola). So maybe is high time we set things right, Mr. Chris, and take you down.

THE ORBIS SPIKE, 1610

Rock, ice and sediment tell
their own stories.
They keep this memory:
in 1610, CO^2 levels dipped —
an Orbis Spike marks the martyred
on fields emptied of trees, emptied
of the dead that could no more labour.
Breathing hectares &
breathing lungs — limbs of bark & limbs
of flesh. No more alive.
Some tell that living wreaths sprung
upon the un-grieved
to cover, as love will, a vast
and crude nakedness,
and shamanic leaves sucked away
that sick era's poison
like unsolicited forgiveness.
Air was breath again;
but never-ever the same.
An infinite absence remains.
     Now, uncaring, we strip ourselves
and call that development.
Forests burn like cancerous lungs
and First Nations are still
the first to die.
     Ancients say, the land breathes for us,
and we for the land.
     Today, I plant a poem.
I put its roots down in soil
brown as cosmic dust.
With every you encircled in every cell,
I ask for a multiplication of leaves —
and for First-Garden breeze.

   Dear Earth,
we have grown so apart.
Now that we are full-blown, obscenely
anthropocene, will you forgive, allow us, again,
to breathe. . .

IBISES AT THE CARONI BIRD SANCTUARY

     Soon red will leak
from their feathers. Already,
crimson creeps seaward.
Already, they are a delicacy – just ten
is enough to make a meal belched
at complicit tables.

Native, local, national –
those proud and tortured tags they suffer,
being covenanted to returns
like migrants starved of rest
and home.

At evening, flocks appear,
spotting the mangroves with multiple stigmata,
until night cloisters all
to morning, when the air is fired
with arrowed flocks.

Many head for the *Main*,
still pristine, and fuller now
of what feeds and coats them.
At dusk, they race back,
brief sojourners gauging home,
like angels to a preferred heaven –
an island that greets
     and targets them.

ORANGE TURN

The Red House has lost its burn,
is now neither dragon nor dove,
this nor that. It's no news;
we've opted to play
the party game: red then yellow
and red again.
It's more of a fête that way,
and that's who we say we are.
All the way to voting day,
party people partying to soca
pumped from trucks, waving
and juggling yellow sun and red flower,
the proverbial garden myth –
paradise, inclusive of its snakes.

This rounds we're under the flower,
and we're not so much happy
as resigned to the turnover:
one day for Peter, one day for…
We know the drill: no one is ever a liar,
no one a thief – and no better.
What to do?
They keep us going – the parties.
They keep us moving –
following direction.
Truth is: we're orbiting the same pole –
treasury bandits, charlatans and blame pushers.
It's hard to tell which is which;
but every four years,
we're far from colour blind
when racing to the finish line.
For clarity, they top us up on promises,
handouts, ten-day work stints, and the latest toy:
new highways to kill time in one-way traffic,

drunk on CO and fixed
on the next mortgage payment,
light bill, or lime.
We toe the line as seasons turn
when there's no real choice to choose.

So we doing it again
with the "great" party in charge
and behind the scenes,
the sun is planning a comeback.
That's the sum of it: one or the other.
We're moving on – and my neighbour
is painting an orange gate
as the ice-cream man peddles past
jingling a familiar bell.

BONES
(for Andrea Bharatt)

No truth is ever buried. Not completely.
Even dry bones live on…

The eternal racket they make
        like a ball and chain blues
playing on the brain.

They turn the dead conscience over,
burrow down to the dark known,

inch their way to surface
to leave small clues on pathways
like resting commas.

They remain with us – the disappeared ones,
holding to stubborn visibility,

awaiting the day
when someone finds a fragment
of the whole.

That day,
flesh will grow on dry bones.

The dead do not easily disappear

GONE VIRAL

Some words return to haunt us at the root.
The world reels from an underrated flu – *gone viral*,
as when a presidential gaffe becomes a kind of math.
Exponential: *Many people will die who have never died before.*
A macabre riff off a space adventure.
Never mind. We're strategising for survival,
strip-searching every sneeze
for an invisible assassin suited in capsid,
ticketed for travel across paper borders,
busy making manic copies of itself.
Toute bagai: we're masked and sanitized,
certified social-distancing compliant,
as best we can, with differences
no virus entirely respects.
All things being far from equal,
we're in this together, at home,
and growing a little familiarity-frayed,
more than a little rectangular-visioned,
and hopefully all in sync that sani-wiping
each other's passage is no way to live;
      but it'll do, for now.
We want to escape the boxed lines
of the taken whatever percent. We want to be here –
for the good of the change,
for whatever beckons beyond survival,
more convinced that virtual chatting
is an imperfect saviour for withholding the best
that presence gives.
      So with no path entirely clear
to the chimerical *new normal,*
we settle for a chance to breathe,
more gracefully, air that was never as clean
as when highways ran empty,
and the sky was once again
      an ascension of birds.

SURVIVAL

Any number of days is one too many
when home is no safe haven against the death
that roams neighbourhood streets,
coughs on a public bus,
reaches for toothpaste on a grocery shelf,
jogs by in less friendly parks…

Any day is one too many
when quarantine thins to a shell
as you are cooking eggs;
so you tiptoe, phantasmal, through a minefield
to quieten house-wearied children,
and trip on your daughter's no nonsense rhyme:
Jumbie-jumbie fly away. Live to fight
another day.

Any minute is one too many
when the masked distance we keep
to flatten the curve and beat down a virus
is a double-barrelled sentence
for one woman too many.

For the one too few, survival
during a pandemic may mean
the helpline that you dial four-eyed,
terror ticking in your veins,
or, in another pocket of the globe,
tremble a whisper to a pharmacist,
Mask 19 please –
all before the one second
when the room, like a bashed wave
explodes…

DESIGN

She'd chosen them carefully – the patio tiles.
Vermont Rust was an abstract mix of browns
interrupted by meandering streams
and basins of blue marble quartz, in matte.
The contractor explained the design
to the tileman that was first made clear to him:
a frontal view of an earth and water landscape.
The man nodded vigorously and at end said,
No problem with a tumbling *r* that revealed him.
She asked his country. *Cuba,* he replied, the *ku*
delightfully cooed. Her anglicized intonation
sounded a suppression; but as he set to work,
she glimpsed a guarded look.
He was far from home and working
for those at home – maybe three times over.
      The contractor left for another site
and she left him to his tiling,
a modest six by four space, but a world
in a time of lockdown.
Later, when he called from the yard, *Mira lady*,
she returned, saw, and said, *Perfecto*,
trying out his lingo. A mask lifted.
He showed his smile and she hers.
She had no heart to object to what appeared
an unintended vulnerability. On the left
was a landscape with its rivers, and on the right,
an ocean washed westwards –
back to his island.

A FUTURE

A neighbourhood in quarantine:
we're most all at home, in *sleep mode*,
playing dead to dodge a virus like a bullet
that no bullet can kill;
even so we're at war 24/7, roaming rooms
between pjs and home-clothes,
front doors and windows open
to views of neighbours puttering about yards,
a little self-consciously, like newcomers to their spaces,
all fugitives from the world beyond our gates,
all refugees from ourselves;
we're weapon and target, victim and cause –
the perfect storm.

In the cool of the evening, no one objects when a father
from the neighbouring street chances a quick turn
with his daughter hoisted on his shoulders.
She looks happy to see beyond herself.
We do not warn, knowing too well
that we've failed her. The world is falling
and the future we hope to somehow make better is hers.

NEGOTIATING WITH A PENDING EARTHQUAKE

(The "big one is coming and it is better to be prepared."
— Seismic Research Centre, St Augustine, Trinidad)

We are dust. Like grass we disappear.
So pending your arrival, we name you Ciba, Rock –
be stable ground beneath us
while we fool ourselves, think ourselves movers
and shakers of worlds, builders of civilizations,
clever designers of skyscrapers that bend and
twist to off-the-chart seismic hits.
We've been warned. August 21st, 2018: Port of Spain
felt your eyebrow twitch.
An awakening is approaching; but please,
please be still.

We're not good with promises,
but we will walk lightly upon the earth. We will cease gobbling
chunks of ground – drilling, digging, extracting.
Is any of this relevant? Will you be sated
if we dispense with bombs charged to shift orbits?
No more blood-washed streets.
We will replenish. Clean. Cool the air.
We will scour hate from our tongues.
We will wash greed from our eyes.
Criminals who eat children
will give proper account.

Please tell us what will make you happy.
We're mere pebbles in your palms,
and these, we know, are children's prayers;
but there's nothing like helplessness
to make intentions pure.
So we pledge to remember the day
the temple's veil was torn;

Ayiti 2010 and her countless dead.
Please, do not forget how easily we're crushed —
flesh and bone.
The miracle of a day's end is enough
to toast ourselves,
boast of the Goliaths we've felled,
Anancies we eluded, Samaritans we helped.
We want to hug our children, cook a meal,
sit in a chair uncomplaining of our weight.
Sigh contentment. Settle.
      Earth is restless.
Glaciers are migrating. Coastlines
are reinventing themselves, human caravans
cross deserts, burning one footstep at a time
to meet a wall some dream to scale or shout down,
and bagged drowned necklace our beaches
while the shivering saved, blanketed in emergency red,
warm on deck. And now,
and now, a pandemic shakes us — indifferent
to our wanting to be where we are
and going where we desire.

Ciba, it is night now. It is enough
that we are mere commas in each other's arms,
moving and trembling together; enough to feel
the stillness of a sleeping house.
We can hear your breathing.
With the slightest shift of opposite plates,
crusts break. Shock — aftershock.
One day, we know, you will awake
and show your motion: nemesis/
science/cross of location.
For now — for one more day, month, year,
decade, please be only, Rock.
On this nearer surface,
we will mark our transience
and dreams of close gods.

HAYA

Here's what we'll do:
I'll take the dirt,
mud, clay – whatever.
No need to get antsy.
The entire story has been yours
for aeons.
That should count for something.
Look at the world you've created.
We've spun killing divides
that turn like palindromic eves.
Now, here's the deal:
you've got the pair
nicely excised, breathing
and multiplied.
We've survived!
So let's not make a stink.
Like I said,
I'll take the mud.
You've got the rib well-cooked.
I get it:
it's a 24/7 job to guard the lines,
which is OK.
In fact, great!
I'm not running your race.
Earth suits me fine.
It's pliable and takes my shape.
Most of all,
that's where stars reside.
So I'm good
with the dirt.

ii: mapping home (en route)...

VALENCIA (EN ROUTE)

The car speeds along an asphalt rollercoaster
with less joy than I remember.
        Valencia.
O Valencia – those gliding syllables
are green undulate valleys
where light glows in steep tabernacles
that shower verdant air tuned to joy-cries of birds
and clapping streams.
        Who remembers that your name's double echoes
a not-too-far bitter history,
or that your land was freedom country
from a war still bellowing its cause, *Black Lives Matter*,
at a stalled liberty?
        O Valencia, that imagined light
before the loss was a luminescence
so without price,
its spectre became compass
        and a genuflection to a ghost –
almost poetic.

Listen:
chainsaws eat at the necks of giants
and the eternal strain of trucks
that ply pocked roads with their guilt-burden groans
a requiem for the splayed land.
Look:
ruptures, voids pierced by lances of denuded rays
strike at an earth we pillage each day
to build us a brand-new world.
        All this light
is so much a hurt. Its fierce flourish
no garden dream,
no shield against the valley's gutted womb;
so omission is the blinkered gaze I choose of late,

pelting all the way through to Matura,
as though fleeing a phantom dark.

The same uneasy divides intrude:
            the sanctuary's fabled whole or
the loss that teaches the pierced heart
            to love
and tips always to an enduring real,
as when the blaze of sun on a single leaf
expands a narrowed horizon
barred against grief.
        What astonishes, and this is no ideal,
is that road through Valencia triggers rage,
like the violation of a temple,
and my vaulted memory of that imagined first
(now receding) shade of green,
like a missed step, burns to cinders.
            All else falls away –
and leaves what first
and always must be loved.

SALYBIA

I do not always veer right off the way
at the sharp turn that leads to Salybia Bay,
and, leaving the car behind
like a castoff encumbrance,
walk along the riverbank's shady aisle
to the screened stretch of beach.
I do not always stop among the believers;
but on approaching the bridge –
so wide it seems a stage –
I slow for a strained view of the bay
that lies beyond the precast slabs of concrete
that serve as rails.
I want to see the worshippers
in their bright cottons that fuse to a cosmic prism
where sea and river greet.
Anticipation is belief enough.
Even when the estuary is empty, they are there,
a vibrant kingdom wedded to a ground
and first ancestor origins sequestered in a name.
No brick and mortar need stake claim
to that everlasting cathedral on the sand.

BALANDRA POUI

Balandra stretch is usually a fly-by to Rampanalgas,
unless you are interested in taking the road
that leads to where fishing boats anchor.
      Today is different.
Across from the bay's entrance, a golden poui
in all her glory interrupts the road's agenda.
Blossoms blaze against a cirrus and blue sky.
You reach for your phone,
hit the camera icon and click twice
to be sure you have the best shot
of what cannot be captured –
a singular beauty, so completely herself.
      You take one last look
before you rejoin the road's flow,
and a Goodison poem surfaces, loops you back
to a dress of fallen flowers
shamelessly tangled about the ankles.
In an instant, that solitary tree,
in full possession of her blossoms,
is changed, forever.

SIMPLY, RAMPANALGAS

Whatever real and storied etymologies
are veiled in the tin-pan clatter
and gallop of its cadence, Rampanalgas,
for the traveller, now conjures a name
no more valiant than the roots that stay this coast:
Arthur's, a one-stop shop and bar combo
with thriving kitchens at its side, is the oasis
that ends the stretch of road barrelling
from Balandra Bay.
        Long after the shop disappears,
its name's origin will suffer no loss,
will be subject of no query for being found
on the *right* side of history;
but positions change and places, too,
must relearn their names.
        What matters here
are the stories that travel in scant traffic flying up
to Matelot from Grande.
Spilt onto the pavement is an animated mix
of villagers and wayfarers passing through to homes
or holiday houses further up the coast.
Like a ritual pause at statue or station,
they stop more to touch the spirit of the place
than to quench any thirst.
        Talk makes light
and laughter erupts like surf
to dispel any cloud.
Speak the name Walcott: unabashed they ask,
"Who, Keshorn, from up Toco?"
Him they know, their javelin hero,
a trophy upheld. No tall-tale fishermen tell
to lift themselves.
No poem, shining god or leviathan
rises from the deep;

and across the road an untamed seascape,
framed by almond trees, is an open door
to a scene beyond history.
The tousled surf delivers
those glorious *slow horses* advancing on Bathsheba,
and racing them, a wind, salty with travel,
and scented with the ocean's washings,
conjures like a Palaeolithic chant or spell
the drag and reek and grit and grind of a sulphurous opening line,
Miasma, acedia... and you know, Rampanalgas –
elemental, ordinary – is never,
could never be, simple.

CUMANA

Cumana is a name not wholly retrievable.
Those *who came* in such beautiful ships
put its meaning in the grave and left a cross
courage resurrected in the beat of a Baptist's drum –
struck even in the church at Mission.
Those who first baptized these coasts
of drumming sea and tall green remain with us.
They, too, are our dancing ghosts.
On its shores, a cruel age rusts down
cannons of conquest – a disappearance
unnoticed by children who emerge
shining from the sea dripping salt
like leatherbacks. They think nothing
of that surviving noun flung
off tongues with no ear or care
for old inflections, but for the season of *gabilan* –
crib of fresh conversions. Cumana,
an ancestral twin sits on the Main
where a revolution was born, and is here
ever more a place whose sense is made
by what is lived and held in memory,
as only a thing that is true can be.
So at the junction's shop where pasts fade
with the aged and rum-drowned cells of regulars,
China is a nearness villagers keep more alive
than the island *Chinee Frank* dreams;
and below the Anglais Road that spirals up to France,
the Tompire river empties with the tide's level
into a sea where dicey boats race to unburden cargoes
of the century's casualties and hope-seekers –
the grace and shadow of a world, like the pulse
and flow of an unfinished becoming…

PALM TREE JUNCTION

Sundays,
when morning is a wide-open eye,
you see them on spot,
waiting for transport where the road divides
at Palm Tree junction.
The signage points to cul de sacs
at Matelot and Point Galera –
not dead-ends in the ordinary sense,
but places of bucket-put-down decision.
When churchgoers of other communions
are busy orchestrating pots to oldies
piped through Radio Toco,
or arranging the cadence of clothes on lines,
they are on their way to pray –
women with heads wrapped like clouds
and the gait of ships, broad-
belted steadfastness, sturdy
as mountains.
Armed with Bible and bell,
they issue an awareness sharp as pleats,
and in the folds of dresses
finished with embroidered sleeves and fringes
like chapel windows,
children with sleep-tight eyes huddle.
To really see them
is to see brave sovereignty
become a signpost.

AT TOCO'S DEPOT

At Toco's depot, fishermen's boats, full-
bellied with silver harvests, gauge the jetty
to moor with accustomed precision.
They fire instructions at each other,
their language as direct as the light they bring.
The one called Bait greets me, "Mornin Moms",
then throws himself onto a bed of nets
to catch some sleep, cradled by his life's labour.
Today, his friendly marking my age is small pickings.
Something greater dawns that offers an anchor,
calms the worry-waves he'd once read on my face.
True to his word, I'm caught by a life of nurturing words
that will together take the air as a cast-net unfurls,
expands a cosmos and, unburdened of itself, dissolves
to a light right here that is poetry's – luminous, transparent,
      as the converted.

TROIS ROCHES

There is no signage,
so unless you know the village
between Mission and L'Anse Noire,
it could be easily missed – just a place
through to somewhere else.

I did not know, and at my asking,
heard my informant say, Tuahwash
(maybe), a word I had repeated
until I caught its sound and later found
a meaning from a map, Trois Roches.

The bay with its signature three rocks
is overlooked by a plantation-styled resort;
but to villagers indifferent to a language
of estates reshaped on their tongues,
Tua-wash (maybe) makes its own sense,
like a recent sign further along the road
that reads *Sobay,*
a local transcription for a beach
that ends a precipice: *Saut Bay*,
meaning jump, or salt, must have a story.

I heard that women gathered on laundry days
at the river that flows into the bay:
Goin to the well, they said: *Tua-wssh*.
You hear water, syllables working,
cleansing – the song that remains.

L'ANSE NOIRE

Volcanic rock of time's first explosion,
swash and sizzle of a coastal tongue,
I do not know your history, not the all of it.
This stretch of coast battles the beat of waves
and dips down steep paths to coves carved from onyx stone.
Most are inaccessible –
what it means to look from the road's edge
to an unreachable rest.
      I do not know your people,
those who were here from the beginning,
except for what is stored on faces
like ancient waterways, and in words,
though few, that still *carry*...
They came across the meeting of waters
to an island just over there – its paths mapped
by the whisper of travelling feet.
I know nothing, too, of those Tobago runaways,
like rebel Sandy, who legend says *swam*
to Trinidad and anchored
on this ragged and booming coastland,
where at Matura and Grand Riviere
leatherbacks lumber to shore
to lay their futures, weeping oceans
like those *Caribs* at Point Galera
before they leapt into a sea-full of stars.
More than survival lives on this coast.
Along its coiling road, pasts are polished rocks
kissed by the everlasting sea
that companions homes with gardens
where tough hope-flowers grow from cuttings
for will-come tomorrows.

A PIECE OF ADVICE

Miss-lady, my advice – teck it
or leave it – is simple:
throw down dat tree.
I go handle it fuh yuh. I doh stick.
One money an no more worries:
no termite, no more bat, no more leaf to sweep
or clog yuh drains.
I know you like de ambiance, de shade;
but Miss, dat is a sandbox – so pray
no big wind blow your way.
Climate change – yuh never hear?
Even storm bad-mind dese days.
Dem branch goin tuh damage yuh property.
Is good advice I givin – no charge!
Let me cut it down
so when rainy season come,
you have no reason to call me.
Not dat I doh want to see *your* face.
I mean, nice is nice. But like I say,
let me put my saw on it.
Cuttin back branch is temporary.
Idle talk is not me,
an a little common sense
better than big shame.
One money and yuh business fix.
I done size up yuh situation.
It have plenty tree more than dat one
to cool yuh breeze.
What yuh say? Now-fuh-now.
Let me cut it down.

SUNDAY JUSTICE

Sunday morning and sheep,
the usual flock of seven, are in my yard,
inching their way up the hill.
Two trail rope tethers.

The owner watches their ascent
from the ruins pile,
unconcerned that the pasture
he has chosen is not his.

"Mornin," I call.
"This is private property.
You can't graze your sheep here."

He looks at me a little peeved.

"No problem," he says. "But is Covid.
I cyan't go too far.
Stay home restriction."

"Yes, we must all…
so please get them off my land."

He remains where he is.
The sheep chomp away, bleating
as they please, tails flicking *cho-cho*.

"You're trespassing," I blurt out
as if to wake him.

"Okay, lady," he concedes as a buffer
before he asks,

"Who untie dem yesterday – you?"

I do not answer.

"Motor car bounce my sheep," he says,
wilfully even-toned.
He looks towards the wounded one.

I see her limp across the ridge
to a fresh patch of grass.
A lamb skips up behind her.
The male shakes his mane.

"Take them elsewhere
or the police will hear.
They're destroying my plants!"

His calm is defiance enough.

"Sheep is choosy eaters," he says.
They not goin to bother wit' yuh plants, ma'am.
Ease me up, dis one monnin."

The ewe bleats as he turns to leave
and again as I jump fuming into my car
to head for the station.

When I misjudge my turn
and the fender grates against the curb,
the entire hill choruses, "BAA!"

TO THE MOTHERLAND

I've taken to full-bodied wine
on some evenings.

The heart, it seems, favours
what bleeds.

Track west along early
north coast trails and you're there –
at the Gulf's lip.

Over the stepping stones
of islands,

through the Dragon's Mouth,
is an unsung motherland.

I drink not the vintage settled,
as colonies were,
on Great House tables,

but the South American kind,
sown in the soil of struggle

then found revolutions, too,
can be unfree.

I drink mostly fruit pressed
where Neruda sang majestically,

and where Eva's star shone.
Her shadows move a knotted song.

I drink the chalice of a continent
my island was once mistaken for –

an El Dorado sought by conquistadores,
fugitives and shifty Bogarts –

that near south, where Chavez
tabled the poor, and Maduro, some tell,
spun a hell.

Casualties knock at our doors.
Now my home is survival's gold

for a country suffering its becoming,
like a Sabbath cup.

I DREAM OF CUBA

Some nights
when the sea across the road
is a whisper,

and the coast rustles
like scattered shells,
I dream of Cuba.

Most times, a wind
pushing off from Guinea
carries me away.

I've time to take nothing
to cause bring-down
or slow my pace.

Sometimes, I dream
I leave shore charioted
by seven swift steeds.

Sometimes a Berber carpet
woven with Sahara sand
flies me there,

and when I touch ground,
lightning and stars
take root in my hair,

and I'm so happy
to have finally arrived,
I walk through rainbows.

And maybe it's the *son* and
the *rhumba*, the *salsa* in the soil
or the pepper in the lingua,

I begin to step, step
and step, twist and dip, and twirl
until I'm spun

into a handkerchief dress,
brown, and colour-layered,
so my hips move the cosmos.

Usually, I'm on the esplanade
at Malecón where waves drum
the seawall,

or on Havana's baroque plazas
where the young still dance
the hope of revolution —

Fidel, like salt, on the tip
of their tongues. Ché, a name
thunders like a god's.

And everywhere is music
cultivated in struggle and joy
that turns the universe.

Whenever I dream of Cuba,
the moment I arrive,
I earth…

HOMING NOW TO STARDUST

My nephew is globetrotting, again –
back to Europe to places I've never seen.
He's in Oberursel, I hear,
but there's no mention of Camp King.
History is in the backseat.
He's simply a tourist having a great time
and sampling German beer.
Days later, pictures arrive of him in Amsterdam.
He is smiling, casual in jeans, T-shirt
and sunglasses – global street-style.
He flags his origins, his earth,
in the print he sports of a water triangle
that frames palm trees against an evening sky,
like a Gestalt half-willing to be read.
In one shot he stands before a sign
that reads *Mozes en Aäronstraat*.
The Golden Palace is near.
I discover something more.
The street's namesake, a church
of his boyhood catechism, now put aside,
stands in the city's east quarter,
that once bordered a Jewish ghetto.
Distance saves us the loss of small joys,
like finding ourselves in an elsewhere –
the truth he wants to celebrate,
the crimes of that era too great a weight
for backpacking vacations.

His next stop is London – without his companions –
to meet his name's relations.
It is his third time to that island
of haunts and dreams,
a geography he knows, though differently.
The plan is to hop English pubs,

see a football match and visit Stonehenge
to consider a cosmic link –
life beyond ourselves.
He goes there, I think, as to a place
on the margins of his life's daily run,
but it draws him in to find a lost
or missing plot.
He has no colonial angst with the Union Jack.
He doesn't call it that –
only the ordinary hope of a young man
to be welcomed by a father
and to see him smile at him,
well pleased.

Dear nephew,
with the name of a high-priestly line,
the mouth of prophets
and attendants at covenant promises,
I know it is hard work putting aside the past.
Living with shadows is greater pain
than finding the treasure of what's left
after an old horror.
We joke de ole Buckingham
would drown in our Queen's Park Savannah.
No naming they gave us
could ever contain the largeness of islands.

Travel cures imagination,
but home is where we anoint ritual,
like your every-year prance through Port of Spain,
a love, you swear, is greater than the kind
that converts homies to voyagers,
leaving for lands that complete the heart.

So, nephew, I pray for you travelling mercies:
the sweet ache for a chosen place

and the anchorage of stars
that stay their course through all seasons
of routes and uprooting.
May the linkage of hearts be sacrament
and altar enough to mend torn landscapes,
as the oceans awash in us gather back into one
the waves that greet our shores,
here and there, with a parenthetical embrace –
paired halves that post smiles
and their flip side, like the heart's reversals,
changeable as the tides –
and constant, too, as any past
cycles back to love.

ON THE CARONI SWAMP

Getting into the boat is easy.
The girth is wide
and the lagoon at the dock is still,
like dead water, but there is life.
My mother is restoration's age,
quietly happy and eager to mend fences.
She laughs at her late adventure
and begins making friends
as soon as she's settled in,
gregarious as the birds we travel to see.
I am grateful for how easily she draws others
to her light.

We travel arbored channels to an anchorage point
tuned into our camera-bearing guide,
seeing, at first, what he invites –
his statistics dated by some need
to keep the fantasy alive.
               We'd anticipated more
than his showing of familiar things:
a pregnant tree-crab, two brown owls,
both asleep, like the "good" snake
he photographs with rapid-fire,
before his apparent miss:
one blue heron feeding on oysters
fastened to the mangrove's arched trusses.
Next: the muted frenzy of bulbous termites' nests.
            The boat falls flat.

Dusk closes in.

A hush descends louder than the motor's labour
as the boat tunnels through the darkening green.
At its end is an alluring light, like young time.

We enter the unfiltered air of a bay
where flamingos, no more than twelve,
are sighted in the shallows.
The birds are recent dwellers. Not native.
From our distance they seem a miracle:
graceful moko-jumbies walking on water.

        The boat holds –
a loaded dash on the water.
    We keep station, overtaken
as by an unrehearsed benediction,
until the one at the back I call the joker says,
"Sitting ducks" – he means for poachers.
        Then like a flipped page
egrets sail toward the trees and settle in
like rowdy owners.
I remain taken by the flamingos,
mostly for fear they will soon disappear.
The boat bobs, lulled by the commotion
until the guides intervenes: "To your left –
        look dem!"
    The main attraction:
ibises begin sailing in.

As light wanes, the first flock approaches
bunched like a fussy mantilla.
They descend to green on a trail of Aaaahs!
My mother sits back, happy to be there,
focusing on the beauty.
She passes around binoculars.
        They are my father's.
He wanted us to have them –
for better viewing.

        I look without their help,
a little stunned, at my view
of the mangrove's punctured palms,

and the roosting egrets,
delicate communion hosts
that the bush slowly swallows.

Back at port, the boat releases us.
We unwind and weave to the carpark
like landed reptiles amid the brief goodbyes.
In the dim lot, I ask my mother,
"You have everything?"
                Silence cracks, like bone.
"Yes," she says, and walks on, empty-handed,
and with an owl's forward-facing eyes.
I yawn double-jointed as we both slide in,
full of the trip, still supple –
                even without the rib.

POINT CUMANA

Great grandmother, Ma,
I remember you
with the scarce economy that fuels story:
your seldom visits from down-country
where home was an entire town, Rio Claro,
the place you journeyed from,
unannounced, to see a son.
We were children
too possessed by holidays and the sea,
to have time or care for you.

All day you sat on that one peerah
like a murti you never prayed before,
serene and strange.
You never called our names,
but stayed stationed like a hyphen
in the corridor of a house
that opened at one end
to Point Cumana.
On the western side is the sea
that delivered you,
a budding adolescent from a ship,
its name long lost to you,
though not the reason you came
(as if yesterday) – *to marrid he fadda,*
gesturing to the son who wed Africa
and settled on the rim of the Gulf.

Turteen chirren borne to the Pa,
my father conjures fitfully as a quiet man
who spoke to his wife in sweet
and secret Hindi,
and who loved the cinema
for the movies of India.

After the *before*, he became a tailor,
but my father had no name for that time —
would never say indenture.

I was too young to treasure answers
to questions I never asked,
but I remember you, Ma,
a small woman, draped in cotton and sheer,
perpetually pulling a slipped orhni
forward, like a private discipline
to forfend the unspoken,
more than to cover your hair.
Silver, I remember.

You moved in slow music.
Sapatas tock-tocked rounds of the yard
and wrists chimed
to your gathering of leaves. Thyme,
coriander and chadon beni mysteries spiralled
from your reluctant stove-top cooking
that was no chulha for sweetening flavour;
but I never saw you dance,
or the fire that perfumed your clothes.
Your lined face
was an indecipherable script.

So much never asked,
like your name
(you were always, to me,
just Ma).

I bear a name your son gave to my father,
one that was never really his;
a name, too, that was never ever mine —
but Ma, I claim you
as an ocean is the bridge

that connects us
when love makes us who we are…

A MOVEMENT ON TIME

In the years before her death, my grandmother
broke ranks and became a Shouter.
Her old church of wafers and dogmas
could no longer contain her, speak or point
the paths to the God of herself.
Somewhere in a dream, I dreamt she said:
You have to dead before you could live.
Forget about the after. Now is the war.
My grandmother loved as the earth is one
and her living was a movement on time,
a risked becoming. New worlds burst from her
when she married indenture to her story.

Before she died, the woman who swam
with her head above water to keep anchored
to the land, wrote a language beyond finalities
on indigo walls and wore cloths of rebirth.
She is and was a seeing, a land, always land.
When she was buried, the sky delivered Jordan
and her grave pooled to protest rites she'd left
to enter the self that resounded truer
than a past she had battled hard to shed.

After the before is the world without end.
We're released from our histories as hope
is an inflected grammar, an unsettlement, liquid
as the flow of memory – the tense of water.
We move through, a traffic of cells, watchers
for a blood moon, points of light in a night sea.
    The first water is air, rock and dirt –
the body rivers on…

A MAXI TO PORT OF SPAIN

"Port of Spain, cole breeze maxi! Who goin?"
Or something in that vein is his sales pitch –
a freelancer working the Curepe junction,
well sheltered from midday hot-sun
by an ochre umbrella, *house and land* version.
I pass into his promised AC haven
amazed at how symbols follow you around,
like those higher-order messengers we call angels.
When a young couple settles in, cool and fresh
in their new love, a child cradled between them,
I think of Maureen and Keeper,* their fictions
less real than the pair I can give no names,
only be blessed by the sun they radiate,
when the woman calls from her seat, "Mr. Drive,
we not paying you tuh waste time."
He sees in her eyes what he cannot combat
and joins the Priority's flow, the conductor left behind,
his *passage* paid, like a Charon assigned to topside.

*characters in *Curfew Chronicles: a fiction* (2017)

WHEREVER I GO…

there will be an island,
and an ocean will be
what rings me.

We are to the very end
a naming not our own,
though we leave to find

what is left behind
and that holds us,
more than we know,

like a small beach
has the ear of the great sea

and a trillion ebbs
are never without returns.

This flow is the staying,
though we depart.

An oyster takes a single grain
and stores it in her heart's muscle

like a lover's memento;
she never lets us go…

iii: saving your fire...

NO / LANGUAGE IS A VIRUS

so I'd rather hear your name and
see your face
that this world may be its fullness,
and not rot away
at the mercy of a flying worm
coded for death.

Words fly the grave, steal
the only thunder a virus can claim,
and, alive,
witness to goodness that quietly thrives.

Always, language re-greens,
     flowers,
exactly when a virus conspires
to lock us down,
chained and metered
to targeted cliches: marked *criminal*,
for running while Black, dangerous for breathing
though we cannot breathe;
     marked *illegal*, *migrant* —
liabilities at borders of fleeting dreams
and on the sea's treacherous table;
marked *wired unblessed* for being
of light — ourselves.
There's a world without end
that prefers us packaged clones,
dispirited, mumbling creeds
like children at their prayers.

I bear a word worn through and
through by the warring centuries,
but faithfully remains to meet us
in this fevered now

      of apotropaic faces
and bodies that girth
six feet separate.
With the many, I too speak it
as prevention's cure for whatever sucks
the air between us,
      lurks in the storehouses of old
and new vocabularies, sentences
and graveyard grammars…

Here: I lift it up like sunlight on raindrops
              — love. Can we bridge with it
to a land, new-minted?

If *language is a virus,*
let poetry be antidote to mend divides,
neutralize frictions, cause upset
to the anatomy of sound & sense
to oust diseased alphabets one *yard*,
one *odyssey*, one slur
and poisoned syllable at a time.

What we exile will, in time,
return like waves *tire of horizons*
at their urgent homecomings,
or prosper,
      indifferent as rage.

No / language is a virus wholly cured…

THE DAWN-BRINGER'S TALE, RETOLD

      Stories are not sky.
None is so high as to speak a last word.
Nothing is ever finished until your part is spoken.
Some stories are not brave enough
for you, or me;
      so, granddaughter,
we must make them braver than the edge
they fear falling over;
make them wider than a horizon
washed of shades,
and patrolled by monsters.

This is my telling of the dawn-bringer:
      One time, second daughter
was travelling through deep forest
with her people when night came.
Father, mother, sisters huddled in darkness,
with danger lurking.
Certain that first daughter was *pure,*
in the necessary way,
the father sent her to bring them back
a small flame from its keeper.
She searched but failed.
Her father's voice barked
so loudly at her heels,
her lover's name darkened the way.
      Not so second daughter:
she banished all shame for her fire
and returned with the entire dawn
from in-dwelling Light-giver.

SOUCOUYANT CONSIDERS FLIGHT

Sometimes it is necessary to tell your version:
Icarus had a sister and all three were in the labyrinth,
bedazzled, when a feather alighted from an unseen heaven
and settled in her father's cup of fever-grass tea,
honey-sweetened thanks to some settler bees.
An idea came: waxed wings. The dilemma:
if only two could fly, who gets left behind?
Daedalus asked for a second cup – to deliberate.
    Of course, Icarus won the ticket up.
He felt, first, the rush of space and saw the lure
of light and, feeling his power veered
from the consigned middle line,
forgot that he was so poorly rigged.
    Yes, the small splash in Brueghel's flat sea
was he. Who cares? She did.
For seeing him tumble to ground in meltdown,
she discovered the trick
as she flung to sky that ball of twine
her father had left behind.
    To save herself, she must become, herself,
  a flying orb of flame.
Fuck Theseus and the Minotaur.

LA DIABLESSE RESURRECT

Night. Full face of moon. Silver.
Madness. Silhouetted. In any hemisphere,
jumbie hour is real-time horror.

Tonight, she is somebody's daughter
trafficked across oceans, flesh supplied
for soul-eaters who pay taxes, harbour

allegiances, kiss their children, talk
of heaven and return to a home,
somebody's showered hero.

Somewhere, she's living contraband
in a wilderness of burdened mattresses,
and unyielding floors, numbed up

that mountain. Her face averted,
she sees through pane and cover of trees
a scaffolded sky her tomorrow's climb.

Then, one redemption night,
La Diablesse-self resurrect to walk
the plantations of the world.

Demon-woman with danger
under her dress, hunter, hunting you.
Watch how vile cow-foot appears

from the abyss of your crime –
a hydra network and devil-demand
that target her. Who is *she*?

The one of many who escapes you,
lives to swallow you like a plunge off
that cliff… the hell you fall into sinew

by sinew. It is SHE who eats you,
retributive jaws of death, flesh
for flesh, cell by cell.

Brand her gothic, if you want —
every origin has its ghosts,
and the terror our pages host

only pale imaginings:
no more than a paltry recall
      of her lived horror.

PERSEPHONE EXPLAINS TO DEMETER

I never chose, mother,
but I see there's a world to uphold.
Seasons to turn. Blah-blah.
I hear megatons babble your words.
A groan since time immemorial…
That's how the world turns,
so-get-on-with-it…
Did you know I went from red
to blue? Let me explain hell.
You wear blue after red. Flame
until you're changed – orange
yellow green, maybe;
you go until almost black, blue-
black, but with a sheen.
      Now I seldom think in pastels.
They're too innocent. Delicate –
like eleven o'clock flowers.
Red. Blue is the after.
Colours can mean so many things –
hot red, yellow butter, cocoa brown,
black gold.
      Between us,
it was mostly black and blue
until white. Blank.
      Nothing.
No place for a long-term stay.
Some days it rained,
but the air dries quickly.
No sense crying.
      I met others there.
We shared and decided on
the necessity of red – an apocalypse
for the most part.
      Then, it happened:

I must warn you, this isn't pretty.
I curved silver and said new prayers.
Not those that stole your tongue
whenever god had an opinion,
or worse, when you settled

to save yourself from meltdown.
Maybe that's too harsh.
You did manage a deal.
The truth is: that was my first cue
to run like hell from your deals;
but not even fields are safe.
The ground caved.
    To this day,
I'm relearning colours.
What I most want
is that they be themselves;
but for now, I need metaphors.
They don't mince matters.
Red to blue.
So going forward,
I'll be elsewhere.
You see, I've relocated where the sun
always shines.
I don't mind flaming from red
to blue – not quite sky;
more a movement to indigo,
the Paramin kind.

    The best way to kill a devil
is to become one.
        Here's the uptake:
I'll need less down time and ash
makes for richer soil.
        Like I said, I'm the knife.

GLEANINGS ABOUT MARIANNE MOORE APPROACHING 1947

Tucked away in cryptic
encyclopaedic lines

that soar like rare
bright birds in the scarce
branched mind,

or jerboas
negotiating a labyrinth,
their truths indirect or flippant
as *cookie dust*,

otherwise, torpedoed ironies,
elegant expletives, clarities
that explode planets
leaving us
satisfyingly startled, schooled,
happily perplexed,

or incisively dismantled
and frazzled, as after a hurricane,

is a leaping cry,

stifled there
        so silent to be keenly felt:

O Mother,
my dearest mother,

rib in my side
as I slept crammed
into a sky-
box with undersized wings,

fed anorexic
on leftover sardines –
while you lived to frown and gnaw
at my script,
lurk behind my every love
until my sex
was cloaked in a casket

that you might sleep
a good night's sleep…

Mother, for forty days
and forty nights, my grief
will be
the unlevelled motion
of water.

When you and I are
done,

and I am
finally
singular,

there will be sun
and a beach flung wild
with stars.

I will walk on it,
my backside rolling to rattle
all the sharks.

I will, sweet mother,
goodbye,
I will…

RELEASING JUDITH'S LINES

Ashes thrown off, I wash, dress,
in clean robes that my land may step out
like a terrible beauty fixed fast on saving
what is infinitely precious – in us,
like the miracle of a leaf is the never-
before-script of each human palm.

Let Judith be born in the blood
of those thrown beneath the unjust press
of any death-breathing Holofernes.
Let her go out into the fields, cities and streets
encamped by all manner of fear and bring-down.
Let her go as one released from the womb of a vast Love
that nourishes and bejewels her with mighty favour.
May her hands, high-commissioned, sever
death's stranglehold.

MISS MILES, ELEVATED

Dear Miss Miles,
      you may not know me. I was just a girl
with no real girlhood
when you took up your suffering road,
and I suppose, ever since you've crossed over,
your ears are full with every type of grief and woe.
It seems we're a slow lot to learn.
So excuse the intrusion,
but I want to tell you, personal,
that since Mr Hall and Miss Cecilia dusted
and polished your memory,
and you danced our streets, thanks to Minsh,
you've never been more real to me;
and maybe I'm a dreamer,
but I've seen your rising star.
              It is so like you, Miss Miles,
cutting style, decked in jewelled night –
no longer that maligned and riddled lady-blue
after Port of Spain was done with you.
Moved-up to top table, you are warrior-
woman of the world, heart-tester,
midnight robber in a hat brimmed wide as Saturn's rings.
All that stamp-down dirt and back-stab shards
must have spun into a halo.
             Ah, Miss Miles, no smell-rose-
good-girl, you sit that hat side-angled, emblem
of those lying streets that sidled when you passed – a city,
you saw, up-tilted like a bottle.
      Who would've guessed?
You, who loved enough to bleed,
were scattered by a lavish hand
as hundred-fold harvest seed.

REMEMBERING ANSON G.

    You are ever more —
to me, a new world Fergus,
who left behind nation rants
to gain rare mystic's passage
through the narrow gate
of sleep and wake.
    For that up-ladder state,
you hewed a craft of blood-
-from-stone living
and stitched a sail of pressed-
down-no thanks-giving,
then set out for the stars.
    Minister Anson,
maybe I've made too little
of my dreams,
though once you bid me
write them down,
if only to decipher clues
for cross-over seasons.
    I never did,
preferring more to labour
at dreaming up poems.
The good news: my nights,
of late, are indigo blue
and pinned with stars,
like I imagine how saints
look down and nod us on.
    One in particular
is extra bright above highlands
like Dylan's Cambrians,
or were they the mountains north
of 1# Sapphire, in August,
or those bluffs,
now to my new south?

I cannot be sure —
your last September
scattered you
like a thousand suns.

FOR ERIC ROACH

    Dear Eric,
I write (now) because I sense you've finally grown,
how shall I say, more reachable. Not that the distance
was ever entirely yours.
    If anything, you wanted to draw near,
be grace for islands, believing that art gathers us in
& at its best stays with us.
I believe there was a welcome you most desired,
and sought to make of verse that mirrored-Self,
not just true, but what you hoped to better love,
all its parts – the real task that slipped from you
mercurial like the ebb of tides.
    You lived best in your verse – fruit
of your patient and pained genuflection
before our fractured beauty and your own torn
or tortured sensibility that laboured
to mend itself with a fierce love for islands
and a studious awe of a canon
that whipped you like a borrowed faith,
though you swore allegiance only to the wind,
but always, always at your heels,
were the jaws of an irreparable chasm
between mask and mirror –
and your creeping disappearance.
    Maybe it was better to have cursed
like a raving Caliban, to have treasured less
the artefact of the line than its free-spirited turning
to a new and coming beat of life,
so that your strict and graceful script
could find its dance, keep step
with the archipelagic wholeness of islands
you so venerated, but were no cure for a dark leaning
that tipped you to *oblivion*.
    Did you believe? Could you

in the wreck of centres find & hold your ground?
      Look – this weeping and exultant geography
even now groans a brave unleashed metre
against the shuttered soul.
True, in this carnage and demon season
when the dead must accuse us,
we live with their bones like our own,
and the fallen shuffle like shattered shells
on the sea's bed.
      But, Eric, there are those who birth
and howl out new words; christen them a faith,
breathe life into bones and watch them stretch out
with backbones like teak and mora
towards fragile tomorrows –
stars never too high to set the sky on fire.
      These islands, you no doubt loved
to your last breath, and carried in your naked palms,
aflame, as at the first eruption that scattered us
into a broken chain – that holding was a world,
histories and continents you fought to solder
against the terror of failure, as the marriage of atoms
makes a new star; and yours, dear poet,
was a miraculous becoming
that left us, unfinished.
      I wanted to tell you, I've been listening
to the gentle shuttle of that ocean
you entered at Quinam.
She speaks of your coming to her without sorrow
and, like a mother, so caressed and turned you over,
she releases you ever more alive.
You will be happy to know, we still reap your words
like a harvest without season,
and as the sea each night beholds its shining orbs,
they yet stir wonder.
I've being trying to figure you – a flowering rock,
moved up to bright crystal.

So rest well. We are all here – under star-gaze,
keeping the faith.

PUT AWAY BLUES

Carnival Tuesday,
by Lapeyrouse Cemetery,
three o'clock sun
blazing hot,

I see a blue moko-jumbie,
sit down on a wall –
        face full-a-worry.

With de music
pumpin,
an de people
jammin,
de band is a mighty river
      flowin-flowin.

Dat one god alone
sit down on a ledge,
back to tombstone,
proppin sorrow
like big-doubt
put a hold on tomorrow,

  though de riddim, de riddim
is life, de street alive
wit' ten thousand feet
crushin strife,
an in every mouth is a song
to put away lie
and beat down.

But blue as de weight
of a world,
dat power sit down

heavy-heavy
on de side ah de road,
just watchin,
as de band keep on movin,
an people dancin,
singin
to foreday mornin.

I see dat one jumbie
jus' lookin

till de people's soca
was one mighty healin,
and jus-so Moko put away mournin,
an light as air, I swear —
I tellin yuh flat
I
        see GOD
I see
Moko-jumbie
        touch ground &
reach sky
                and move on…

LEGACY

The lady-poet makes recordings of her last poems
with the windows open to a singing mango tree
that overhangs her yard.

She reads as the washing machine turns,
out-pacing an interrupted *normal.*
Endless stay-in days that gather weight.

She pauses as sirens wail after a car caught,
she imagines, on an *essential trip,* speakers booming
Machel's latest hit, *I Love You,* at subdued houses.

Through salt hours that heap the climbing dead,
she delivers lines with gravel in her throat.
Her breath is near, and warm, as she reads

to a passing world we know little how to mourn,
caring for all and nothing but to leave behind a voice,
as masked mouths touting *recovery* hog screens
and fog up precious vision when they speak.

PLEASE SEND ME FLOWERS

What if, today, I write this line,
         hesitant
as an indulgent hypothetical
in a dark time:
if ever I asked for anything,
it would be this: Please send me flowers.
    Especially now,
when death storms down on a people
everyday robbed of ground;
when across the hemispheres screens flash
cratered earth, bloodied petals, snapped stems,
wailing roots, grotesque blossoms, someone's beloved –
will it make me, too, colonial,
if *colonizers write about flowers?*

    Today, of all days,
I want no wreaths near,
none of those reluctant showpieces
that sit in hospitals.
    Send me blossoms from my landscape,
uncut brilliance – ixora, heliconia, hibiscus,
bougainvillea fortified with sunlight.
Send hosts – ten thousand-thousand –
and if push comes to shove,
even those deserving of the metaphorical kick.

    What if in my geography
all flowers are roses
and I knew no litany of names?
    I ask simply for roses,
any kind, from any soil,
    every perfume and hue,
released from tyrannical histories.
I welcome each with a zillion thanks,

push aside my clutter: my grief, my rage, my fear,
all my abstractions, to make room
                front and centre
just for them and, for a moment,
behold each fragile life,
let them all breathe, be light,
allow their glory to greet my shadowed corners
in this my world –
its betrayals, brutalities, murders.

I write about flowers now,
when a colonizer is flattening a country;
I want to have near what is beautiful
as flowers are beautiful and, like a new moon,
signal turning seasons.
        Will I have done nothing for Gaza
to be a poet from a region, a history,
where remaking style has always been life – thunder
in a world, an Order
that tries but has failed
to make ghosts of us…?
        Palestine, your flowers must be yours.

LOVING THE DAFFODILS

i have tried. i have & i do
love them – the daffodils. Yes,
they know nothing
of the histories they carry. I do &
i love them
like i love all roses, tulips, irises,
chrysanthemums… I understand –
journeys can be tough.
i too have strolled along spring streets
with a bright bouquet cradled in my arm,
like something ever so precious.
Nothing compares to their particular shade
of yellow. Sunshine, maybe;
but metaphors are tricky at playing dead.
I've sat in my brown-
black skin, with them in vases
at four o'clock tea, serving the sweet.
They do cheer up a room.
One day, someone else, another
generation may forget
how much history we carry. I've tried
to love them historyless.
I've even wondered if they too remember.
i do
forgive what's there to forgive. Memory
though has those unpredictable fits.
I cannot, not yet, forget;
but i do love them – the daffodils,
after all, are simply flowers, beautiful –
handsome as any…

RETURNS

Once, I asked an artist to paint me a cover
for my then last book.
Instead, after a reading,
he left me an image from a poet
whose name he couldn't remember.

He described a swimmer
signalling to the shore from far out
in deep water.
That day, those who saw, but could not hear,
thought the swimmer not drowning
but waving.
His words, a millstone, hung at my neck.

In the end, my book was nicely suited
in shutterstock; and I discovered,
she had a greater ambition than sinking.
      Last time I looked, she's still afloat
and making waves with each turned page.
I know, now, that all my life
I've been trying to rescue her –
but no more.
She's a strong swimmer.
      We make our own returns.

ABOUT THE AUTHOR

Jennifer Rahim is a widely published poet, fiction writer and literary critic. Her poetry collection, *Approaching Sabbaths* (2009) was awarded a prestigious Casa de las Américas Prize in 2010. *Redemption Rain: Poems* was published in 2011 and *Ground Level: Poems* in 2014. *Songster and Other Stories* (2007) was her first well-received collection of short stories. *Curfew Chronicles: A Fiction* (2017), a linked suite of stories, was the winner of the 2018 OCM Bocas Prize. She currently teaches in the Department of Literary, Cultural and Communication Studies at the University of the West Indies, St Augustine, Trinidad.

NOTES

"Please Send Me Flowers" is a response to Noor Hindi's "Fuck your Lecture on Craft, My People are Dying". "Loving the Daffodils" was written after reading Jason Allen-Paisant's "Daffodils (Speculation on Future Blackness)".

ALSO BY JENNIFER RAHIM

Songster and Other Stories
ISBN: 9781845230487; pp. 145; pub. 2007; price £8.99

Rahim's stories move between the present and the past to make sense of the tensions between image and reality in contemporary Trinidad. The contemporary stories show the traditional, communal world in retreat before the forces of local and global capitalism.
   A popular local fisherman is gunned down when he challenges the closure of the beach for a private club catering to white visitors and the new elite; the internet becomes a rare safe place for an AIDS sufferer to articulate her pain; cocaine has become the scourge even of the rural communities. But the stories set thirty years earlier in the narrating 'I's' childhood reveal that the 'old-time' Trinidad was already breaking up. The old pieties about nature symbolised by belief in the presence of the folk-figure of 'Papa Bois' are powerless to prevent the ruthless plunder of the forests; communal stability has already been uprooted by the pulls towards emigration, and any sense that Trinidad was ever edenic is undermined by images of the destructive power of alcohol and the casual presence of paedophilic sexual abuse.
   Rahim's Trinidad, is though, as her final story makes clear, the creation of a writer who has chosen to stay, and she is highly conscious that her perspective is very different from those who have taken home away in a suitcase, or who visit once a year. Her Trinidad is 'not a world in my head like a fantasy', but the island that 'lives and moves in the bloodstream'. Her reflection on the nature of small island life is as fierce and perceptive as Jamaica Kincaid's *A Small Place*, but comes from and arrives at a quite opposite place. What Rahim finds in her island is a certain existential insouciance and the capacity of its people, whatever their material circumstance, to commit to life in the knowledge of its bitter-sweetness.

Curfew Chronicles
ISBN: 9781845233624; pp. 208; pub. 2017, £9.99

Winner of the 2018 OCM Bocas Prize
"This must surely rank as one of the most ambitious books ever attempted by a Caribbean writer. The philosophical, moral and religious themes and ideas put forward about community in all its many manifestations are lightly, deftly handled... Readers are rewarded by moments of sheer grace; and numinous revelations at every turn," Lorna Goodison, chief judge of the 2018 OCM Bocas Prize For Caribbean Literature.

In 2011, the Trinidad government declared a state of emergency and an overnight curfew. The SoE, brought in to combat the crime and killings associated with the drugs trade, was meant to last 15 days but lasted four months. This is the background to these chronicles, but not their substance. They are an imaginative response to the undertones of those days. Taking place over 24 hours, *Curfew Chronicles* brings together, like a Joyce's *Ulysses* in miniature, the lives of two dozen characters (including a father and son searching for each other) whose lives intersect in mostly fortuitous but sometimes quite deliberate ways.

From the Minister and his wife, to those targeted by the state; from those in regular jobs, to those who scuffle for a living on or over the edge of the law; from those who speak out, to the hidden hands prepared to silence them: no one is unaffected by the SoE. What makes these stories individually rich (as well as collectively ingenious) is the depth of characterisation. There is Scholar the street-corner prophet, Ragga with his vision of better days, Keeper tempted into crime to the distress of his redoubtable partner Maureen, Sumintra, the Pentecostal convert struck dumb in prayer, Marcus the assassin whose life is a movie, Amber the security guard and poet and her policeman lover Calvin, eager to retire from clearing up little matters like the "weed" found in the PM's residence, and many more. Each has a resonant backstory; each is caught at a moment of decision or revelation. As these characters criss-cross Trinidad, Rahim builds an unforgettable world of people in a vividly realised landscape.

Between the Fence and the Forest
ISBN: 9781900715270; pp. 88; pub. 2007; price £7.99

Adopting the persona of a douen, a mythical being from the Trinidadian forests whose head and feet face in different directions, Jennifer Rahim's poems explore states of uncertainty both as sources of discomfort and of creative possibility.

The poems explore a Trinidad finely balanced between the forces of rapid urbanisation and the constantly encroaching green chaos of tropical bush, whose turbulence regularly threatens a fragile social order, and whose people, as the descendants of slaves and indentured labourers, are acutely resistant to any threat to clip their wings and fence them in.

In her own life, Rahim explores the contrary urges to a neat security and to an unfettered sense of freedom and her attraction to the forest 'where tallness is not the neighbour's fences/ and bigness is not the swollen houses/ that swallow us all'. It is, though, a place where the bushplanter 'seeing me grow branches/ draws out his cutting steel and slashes my feet/ since girls can never become trees'.

Approaching Sabbaths
ISBN: 9781845231156; pp. 132; pub. 2009; price: £8.99

These poems move seamlessly between the inwardly confessional, an acute sensitivity to the distinctive subjectivities of an immediate circle of family, friends and neighbours, and a powerful sense of Trinidadian place and history. Few have written more movingly or perceptively of what can vex the relationship between daughters and mothers, or with such a mixture of compassion and baffled rage about a daughter's relationship to her father. If Sylvia Plath comes to mind, acknowledged in the poem 'Lady Lazarus in the Sun', the comparison does Rahim no disfavours; Rahim's voice and world is entirely her own. There is in her work a near perfect balance between the disciplined craft of the poems, and their capacity to deal with the most traumatic of experiences in a cool, reflective way. Equally, she has the capacity to make of the ordinary something special and memorable.

This is a work rich in compassion and involvement with other lives.

The threat and reality of fragmentation – of psyche's, of lives, of a nation – is ever present, but the shape and order of the poems provide a saving frame of wholeness. Poem after poem offers phrases of a satisfying weight and appositeness, like the description of the killers of a boy as 'mere children,/ but twisted like neglected fields of cane'.

Winner of a Casa de las Américas Prize 2010 – one of Latin America's oldest and most prestigious literary awards, its jury said that the collection "captures a sense of the complexities of historical, social and cultural aspects of contemporary Caribbean".

Ground Level
ISBN: 9781845232054; pp. 100; pub. 2014; price: £8.99

In 2011 the Government of Trinidad & Tobago declared a state of emergency to counter the violent crime associated with the drugs trade. *Ground Level* confronts the roots of the madness and chaos seething under the surface of this "crude season of curfew from ourselves" when the state becomes a jail. For Rahim, her country is a place where "No-one hears the measure of shadow in any rhythm", a place where "poets hurt enough to die".

In this dread season, Rahim finds hope and consolation in the word and in those places where it is possible to find salvation in "this landscape of ever-opening doorways", such as Grand Riviere, the subject of a long, twelve-part reflection on the values that can still be found in rural Trinidad. Elsewhere she engages in dialogue with those writers who confronted the Janus face of Caribbean creativity and nihilism: writers such as Earl Lovelace, Eric Roach, Victor Questel, Derek Walcott, Kamau Brathwaite and Martin Carter, praying of the last "let his words drop on the conscience of a nation". Alluding to the late Jamaican poet Anthony McNeill, she confides that "The Ungod of things has not changed".

This is an ambitious collection that speaks in both a prophetic and a literary, intertextual voice, which combines the personal and the public in mutually enriching ways; it shows the assurance of a poet who has constantly worked at her craft, but who also takes formal risks to capture the reality of desperate times.